Pergamano®

EYECATCHING DESIGNS

Gerti Hofman

★ Pergamano® is the brand name under which books and materials for the creative hobby Parchment Craft are marketed.

For information about products and/or courses:
Pergamano International
P.O. Box 86
1420 AB Uithoorn
The Netherlands
tel: +31(0)297 522533
fax: +31(0)297 526256
e-mail: info@pergamano.com
internet: www.pergamano.com

ISBN 90-77173-03-x
NUR 475

Translation: The Language Lab, Amsterdam, The Netherlands
Photography: Ferry Herrebrugh, Amstelveen, The Netherlands
Cover: Artnic Creatief Servicebureau, Deventer, The Netherlands
Typesetting: Cees Overvoorde, Utrecht, The Netherlands
Printing: Thieme Deventer, Deventer, The Netherlands

CONTENTS

FOREWORD

Gerti and I go back a long way. Ever since we met I've had the deepest admiration for her beautiful designs and creative output. Over the years, Gerti has developed her own style, which I'm sure not only appeals to me but also to many others. Varied designs featuring extraordinary paintwork, finished with original "lace" borders make Gerti Hofman's book accessible to a large parchment-loving audience.

Gerti, I would like to take this opportunity to thank you for the wonderful time I had working with you. In all those years as a teacher, your courses inspired many people to refine their skills in the beautiful parchment art by showing them the tricks of the trade. Now you've successfully completed your first book and it looks absolutely wonderful. I would like to congratulate you on the result; it will be a source of inspiration for all those who enjoy the unique and versatile quality of parchment craft. This publication will enable everyone around the world to become acquainted with your amazing creativity.

So my advice to the readers is:
"Highly recommended!"

Martha Ospina
Author and President I.P.C.A.

INTRODUCTION

For many years now I've had this great and varied hobby, and I'm not the only one. I share the pleasures of parchment craft with many thousands of people all over the world.

In May 1995 I became a certified Pergamano® teacher, which is when I was introduced to Martha Ospina. Martha really knows how to encourage anyone interested in parchment art to make beautiful objects and develop their artistic skills. This is how she inspired me to make my first designs. I really enjoy contributing to the Pergamano® magazines, to articles for various crafts magazines and, of course, to features in Pergamano World. For many years, it's been my ambition to make my own book and finally I've pulled it off. It has been a true pleasure making these designs and I hope you all will have as much fun working with them.

Gerti Hofman

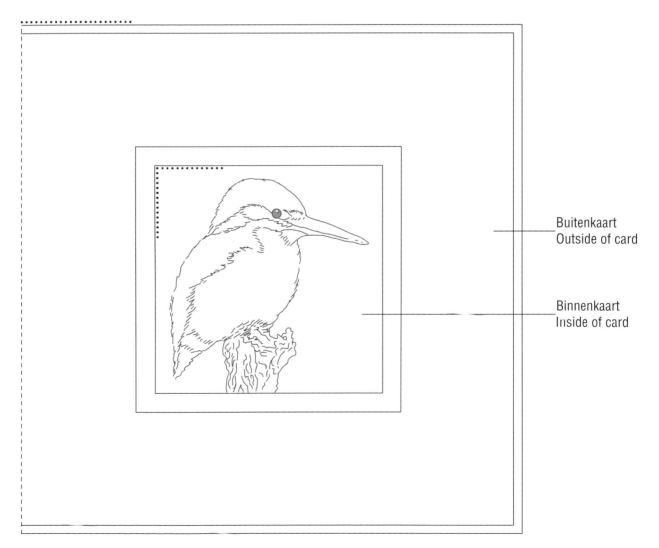

Buitenkaart
Outside of card

Binnenkaart
Inside of card

Pattern Kingfisher (p.34)

ALPINE ANEMONES

General

The card is made of dark green cardboard. The card has three extra front sheets: one of dark green cardboard and two of ordinary parchment paper (on the large extra front sheet you will find a perforation border; the small extra front sheet has the design painted on it). Other materials: mother-of-pearl embroidery thread.

Extra voorblad donkergroen
Extra front dark green

Kaart donkergroen
Card dark green

Klein extra voorblad
Small extra front

Groot extra voorbl
Large extra front

Knippen /Cut out
Borduren /Embroider

Knippen /Cut out

Tracing
On small extra front sheet: Tinta Pearl white (01TP): flowers and outline circle; Tinta Pearl sepia (12TP): dots around flower heart; Tinta Pearl bronze (= Tinta Pearl white (01TP), Tinta Pearl yellow (16TP) and Tinta Pearl sepia (12TP) mixed): stamens.
On large extra front sheet: Tinta Pearl white (01TP): outline circle.

Painting
Tinta Pearl yellow (16TP): balls on stamens; Tinta Pearl sepia (12TP): small dot below balls on stamens.

Perforating (shallow)
With the 4-needle tool according to the pattern of small extra front sheet; with the 4-needle tool and Cross-shaped perforating tool according to the pattern of the large extra front sheet.

Trace a second time
Tinta Pearl yellow (16TP): alternating dots in the centre of Cross-shaped perforations; Tinta Pearl white (01TP): dots between 4-needle and Cross-shaped perforating tool on extra front sheets of ordinary parchment paper according to pattern.

Perga-Liners (dry technique)
B9, B7 and B6 (on front of small extra front sheet): flower hearts; B8, B7 and B6 (on back of small extra front sheet): entire space between the flowers and outline circle.

Embossing
Flowers, flower hearts, balls on stamens, outlines circles and all dots between 4-needle and Cross-shaped perforating tool on extra front sheets of ordinary parchment paper.

Perforating (deep)
With the 4-needle tool once again according to the pattern of small extra front sheet; with the 4-needle tool and Cross-shaped perforating tool again according to pattern of large extra front sheet.

Cutting
Cut Cross-shaped perforations according to pattern; cut outlines circles of extra front sheets of ordinary parchment paper along the outer 4-needle perforations according to pattern.

Finishing off
Attach the small extra front sheet to the large extra front sheet and use the 1-needle tool to perforate within the inner row of the 4-needle perforations. Embroider with the embroidery thread between the 4-needle perforations according to pattern. Attach this to the dark green extra front sheet with double-sided tape. Use the 1-needle tool again to perforate within the inner row 4-needle perforations of the large extra front sheet. Embroider with the embroidery thread between the 4-needle perforations according to pattern. Fold the card and cut to size. Attach the three extra front sheets to the card with double-sided tape.

TULIPS

General
The inner card is made of dark green cardboard, the extra inner card is made of light green Fantasy Parchment 2 (art.no. 1477) and the outer card is made of Parchment Vellum spring (art.no. 1621). Other material: silver peel-off sticker lines, silver embroidery thread and transparent shiny ribbon (about 50cm long).

Tracing on light green Fantasy Parchment
Tinta white (01T): flowers and buds; Tinta leaf green (10T): flower stems and leaves.

Painting
Tinta leaf green (10T) + Pintura green (08): flower stems and leaves.

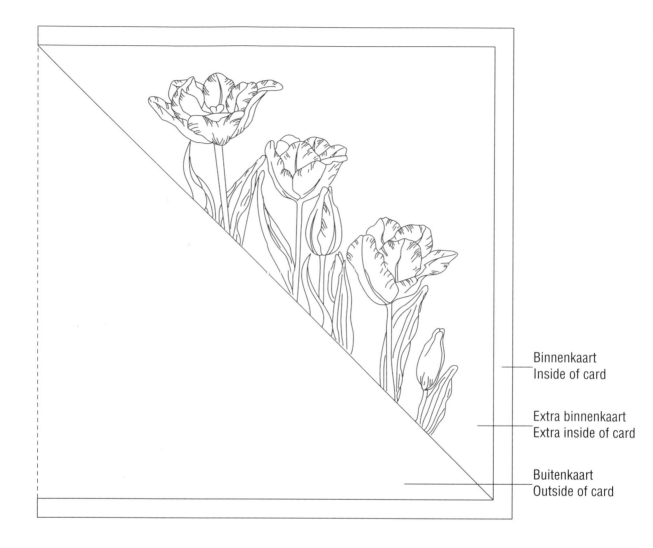

Binnenkaart
Inside of card

Extra binnenkaart
Extra inside of card

Buitenkaart
Outside of card

Embossing
Flowers, buds, flower stems and leaves.

Finishing
Cut the cards to size. Fold the outer card and the two inner cards and thread them together along the fold line with the embroidery thread. Attach the peel-off sticker lines on the front sheet of Parchment Vellum spring and on the front sheet of light green Fantasy Parchment. Tie a bow in the centre van the ribbon, fold the ribbon around the front sheet of the card and attach it on the inside along the fold line with embroidery thread.

ROSE WITH CUTAWAY BORDER

General

The outer card and the 3-D elements are made of Parchment Vellum roses (art.no. 1620) and the inner card is made of white Fantasy Parchment 1 (art.no. 1476). The picture is done on an extra sheet of Parchment Vellum roses (11x11cm) (referred to below as 'extra front sheet'). 3-D elements: rose (consisting of 3 parts). Other material: mother-of-pearl embroidery thread.

Buitenkaart
Outside of card

Extra voorblad
Extra front

1x   1x   1x

Tracing

Tinta white (01T): all 3-D elements.
On extra front sheet: *Tinta white (01T): outline and entire picture.*
On outer card: *Tinta white (01T): flower design in border, card outline and straight lines.*

Perforating (shallow)

On extra front sheet: with 5-needle tool along outline.

Embossing

All 3-D elements.
On extra front sheet: with embossing tool Hockey Stick along outer border van all leaves, rose, buds and stems; with embossing tool Extra Small Ball on outline and between 5-needle perforations according to pattern.
On outer card: flower design in border, card outline and straight lines.

Perga-Liners (dry technique)

B3 and B10: apply shadow on back along bottom of rose, buds, leaves and along right side of stems. First apply very short lines (1 of 2 mm) with B3, then take B10 and trace over the B3 lines and lengthen them slightly (this fades the brown of B3 somewhat). Using the same technique, apply very subtle shadow inside of 3-D elements (on the side that is not embossed). Make sure to keep checking the colour example.

Perforating (deep)

On extra front sheet: with 5-needle tool a second time along outline (swivel tool slightly to left and right).

Cutting

Cut extra front sheet out along outer 5-needle perforations.

Finishing

Fold the inner card and the outer card and thread them together along the fold line with the embroidery thread. Attach the cards firmly to each other with Scotch tape all around. Perforate with the 2-needle tool through the four layers of the card in one try, according to pattern. Cut out the perforated parts and the card outline layer by layer. Attach the extra front sheet on the front sheet of the outer card using the embroidery thread. Use the holes of the 5-needle perforations in the corners. Attach the 3-D elements on the extra front sheet with a dab of Pergakit.

ORANGE TULIPS

General

The outer card is made of ordinary parchment paper, the inner card is made of honey yellow paper (Artoz) and the insert card is made of mango (orange) cardboard (Artoz). Extra material: Gold-coloured embroidery thread and crafts scissors.

Tracing

Tinta gold (22T): all straight lines of front sheet; Tinta orange (06T): tulips, leaves and stems.

Painting

Tinta orange (06T) thinned with water: light parts of tulips, leaves and stems; Tinta orange (06T): parts of tulips, leaves and stems that are slightly darker; Pintura orange (06): shadow on tulips, leaves and stems.

Perforating (shallow)

With 4-needle tool according to pattern.

Trace a second time

Tinta orange (06T): flower shapes and dots in perforation borders; Tinta white (01T): curved lines around 4-needle perforations according to pattern.

Embossing

Tulips, leaves, stems, small flowers and dots between 4-needle perforations according to pattern, straight outlines and curved lines.

Achterblad
Back

Voorblad
Front

Perforating (deep)

With 4-needle tool a second time according to pattern; with 2-needle tool along the outline on both sides of the front sheet.

Cutting

Cut the 4-needle perforations into crosses according to pattern; cut the bottom border of the front sheet out along the outer 4-needle perforations; cut the 2-needle perforations out along the outline on both sides of the front sheet.

Finishing

Paint the cutting border on the outer border of both sides of the front sheet with Tinta gold (22T). Fold the outer card and the inner card and thread them together along the fold line with the embroidery thread. Cut the inner card and the back sheet of the outer card off straight. Attach the insert card with double-sided Scotch tape on the inside of the inner card. Cut a border along the insert card with crafts scissors.

SHELLS

General

The outer card and the inner card are made of ivory Fantasy Parchment 2 (art.no. 1477). Other materials: gold-coloured embroidery thread.

Tracing

Tinta gold (22T): outline, all straight lines, arc lines, shells and parts of shells in the border; Tinta sepia (12T): parts of shells in the centre of the card.

Painting

Shell at top left: Pintura cinnamon (52): upper part; Pintura orange (06) and Pintura cinnamon (52) mixed: bottom part; Pintura brown (12): lines on

shell; Pintura white (01): serrated edge at bottom. *Shell at top middle:* Pintura white (01): narrow edges; Pintura white (01) + dab of Pintura brown (12): areas between narrow edges; Pintura brown (12): shadow lines; Pintura cinnamon (52): spots on narrow edges. *Shell at top right:* Pintura cinnamon (52): upper part; Pintura white (01) + dab of Pintura cinnamon (52): lower part; Tinta white (01T) spots and curled edge upper part; Pintura brown (12): shadow lines upper part and bottom left; Pintura cinnamon (52): shadow lines lower part. *Small shell at left:* Pintura white (01) + dab of Pintura brown (12): right part; Pintura brown (12): lines. *Long shell at left:* Pintura white (01) + dab of Pintura brown (12): upper part; Pintura cinnamon (52): middle part and narrow edge at bottom; Pintura white (01) and Pintura cinnamon (52) mixed: lower part; Pintura cinnamon (52): lines on middle part ; Pintura brown (12): spots and lines on upper and lower part. *Large shell at middle right:* Pintura cinnamon (52) thinned with water: upper part and third part from the top down; Pintura white (01) + dab of Pintura brown (12): second part from the top down and lower part; Pintura cinnamon (52): lines in cinnamon parts; Pintura brown (12): lines on brown parts; Tinta white (01T): vertical lines. *Large shell at bottom left:* Pintura yellow ochre (05) + dab of Pintura cinnamon (52): right part; Pintura cinnamon (52): lines. *Small shell at bottom left:* Pintura white (01) + very small dab of Pintura cinnamon: middle part; Pintura cinnamon (52): sides; Pintura brown (12): lines. *Shell at bottom right:* (see shell at top middle). *Small shell at bottom right:* Pintura cinnamon (52): left part; Pintura brown (12): lines.

Perforating (shallow)
With Semi-Circle perforating tool along outline according to pattern.

Embossing
Outline, all straight lines, arc line and all shells.

Perforating (deep)
With Semi-Circle perforating tool once again along outline according to pattern.

Finishing off
Fold the inner card and the outer card and thread them on the fold line together with the embroidery thread. Perforate with the 2-needle tool along the card outline and cut the card out along these perforations.

GIFT TAG SHELLS

General
The card is made of ordinary parchment paper and the insert card is made of dark blue cardboard (Artoz).

Tracing
Tinta gold (22T): outline, all straight lines and shells in the border; Tinta sepia (12T): large shell.

Painting
Pintura cinnamon (52): large shell; Pintura brown

(12): small shadow lines on lower edge of large shell and on sides at top of large shell.

Perforating (shallow)
With 4-needle tool along card outline according to pattern.

Embossing
Large shell, outline, all straight lines, shells in the border and dots between 4-needle perforations.

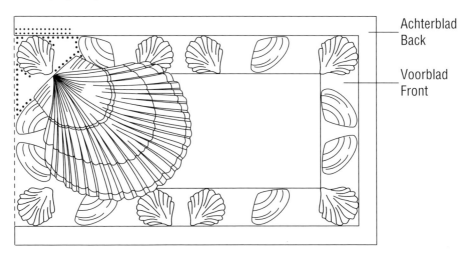

Achterblad
Back

Voorblad
Front

Perforating (deep)

With 4-needle tool a second time along card outline according to pattern; with 2-needle tool between small shells according to pattern.

Cutting

Cut the card out along the outer 4-needle perforations; cut out the 2-needle perforations.

Finishing off

Fold the card. Attach the insert sheet in the card with double-sided tape. Cut the back sheet and the insert sheet off straight.

SEAHORSES

General

The outer card is made of ordinary parchment paper and the inner card is made of dark blue paper (Artoz). Other material: gold-coloured embroidery thread.

Tracing

Tinta white (01T): seahorses and card outline; Tinta gold (22T): shells and outlines of shell border.

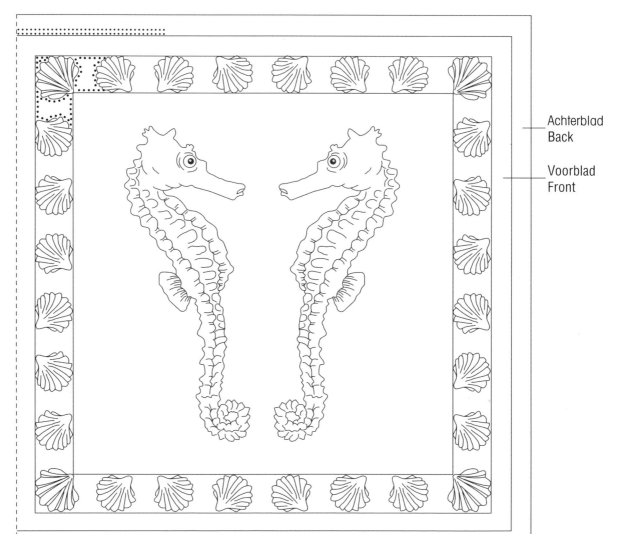

Achterblad
Back

Voorblad
Front

Embossing

Seahorses, shells, card outline and beside golden outlines to create thin white lines.

Perforating

With 2-needle tool parts between shells according to pattern.

Cutting

Cut out 2-needle perforations between shells.

Finishing

Perforate with the 4-needle tool along the card outline. Emboss dots between the 4-needle perforations. Cut the card out along the outer 4-needle perforations. Fold the outer card and the inner card. Thread the cards together along the fold line with the embroidery thread. Cut the inner card and the back sheet of the outer card off straight.

RHODODENDRON

General

The card is made of light green Fantasy Parchment 2 (art.no. 1477). The card has two extra front sheets: one made of light green Fantasy Parchment 2 and one made of ordinary parchment paper with the design painted on it. A light pink sheet of paper has been attached between the two extra front sheets. Other materials: mother-of-pearl embroidery thread.

Tracing

On extra front sheet made of ordinary parchment paper: Tinta leaf green (10T): leaves; Tinta sepia (12T): stems and yellow/brown parts of bud; Tinta white (01T): decorative lines and shapes in border, circle on inside and outside of border.

Painting (with Perga-Liners)

B1, A1, A9 and A8: flowers and pink parts of bud; B8, B9, B3, A20 and A17: yellow/brown parts of bud; B8, B9, B3, A19 and A17: stems; B8, B7, B6, A20, A15 and A16: leaves; B3, A17 and A12: small brown/red leaves below flower bud; B8, B7, A20, A15 and A16: fresh bud; A8: spots on flower; A1 and A2: stamens; A20 and A17: balls on stamens; A17, A12 and A3: fine lines on right side of the stems.

Perforating (shallow)

With 4-needle tool according to pattern of extra front sheets.

Embossing

Flowers, buds, leaves, stems, dots (alternating) between 4-needle perforations in border of the light green extra front sheet and then according to pattern, circle on inside and outside of border, decorative lines (very light) and shapes in the border.

Stippling

With 1-needle tool: circle inside the border and all decorative lines in the border.

Perforating (deep)

With 2-needle tool between decorative lines and shapes in border according to pattern; with 4-needle tool a second time according to pattern of extra front sheets.

Cutting

Cut out the 2-needle perforations between the decorative lines and shapes in the border; cut out the light green extra front sheet along the inner 4-needle perforations according to the pattern; cut out the front sheet of ordinary parchment paper according to the pattern.

Finishing off

Fold the card. Perforate with the 2-needle tool along the card outline and cut the card out along these perforations. Cut the insert sheet to the size of the inner circle and attach the circle on the light green extra front sheet with double-sided tape. Attach the extra front sheet of ordinary parchment paper on the light green extra front sheet with a few stitches of embroidery thread between the 4-needle perforations according to the pattern. Now attach the extra front sheets on the card in one piece with four stitches of embroidery thread (between the 4-needle perforations).

Kaart
Card

Extra voorblad /gewoon perkamentpapier

Extra front /regular parchment paper

Extra voorblad /Fantasie Perkament

Extra front /Fantasy Parchment

Borduren /Embroider

Knippen /Cut out

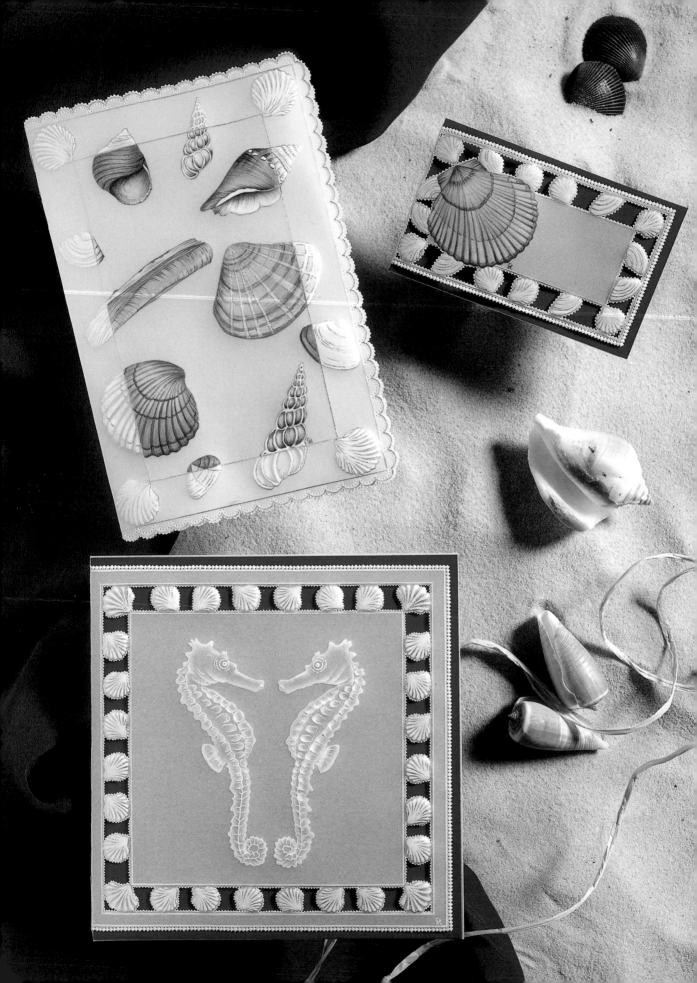

FOXGLOVE

General

The outer card is made of ordinary parchment paper and the inner card is made of light green Fantasy Parchment 2 (art.no. 1477). A pastel yellow sheet of paper was used behind the front sheet of the outer card. Other material: mother-of-pearl embroidery thread.

Binnenkaart
Inside of card

Buitenkaart
Outside of card

Knippen / Cut out

Tracing

Tinta white (01T): flowers and all straight lines; Tinta leaf green (10T): stem, leaves and petals.

Painting (with Perga-Liners)

B1, A1, A9 and A8: bottom five flowers; B1, B8, A1, A19, A9 and A8: other flowers; A8: spots in open flowers; B8, B7, B6, A20, A15 and A16: stem, leaves and petals; A3: highlights on stem and leaves.

Dorsing (with Dorso oil)

Dorso light green (assort. 1): between double lines of borders and between double outlines.

Perforating (shallow)

With perforating tool Flower Tool according to pattern.

Embossing

Flowers, stem, leaves, petals, all straight lines and between Flower Tool perforations according to pattern. Emboss on front: inside of flowers.

Perforating (deep)

With perforating tool Flower Tool a second time according to pattern.

Cutting

Cut Flower Tool perforations out according to pattern.

Finishing

Fold the outer card. Perforate with the 2-needle tool along the card outline and cut the outer card out along these perforations. Fold the inner card. Thread the inner card and the outer card together along the fold line with the embroidery thread. Attach pastel yellow paper behind the front sheet of the outer card with double-sided Scotch tape, but not behind the dorsed green parts between double lines of border and double outlines. Cut the inner card off straight (about 2mm larger than the outer card).

FLY AGARIC

General

The card is made of ivory Fantasy Parchment 2 (art.no. 1477).

Tracing

Tinta white (01T): card outline, all straight lines and leaves in the border; Tinta leaf green (10T): several blades of grass; Tinta sepia (12T): leaves and several blades of grass.

Painting

Tinta orange (06T) and Tinta red (03T) mixed: first layer on red cap of wild mushrooms; Pintura orange (06) and Pintura red (03) mixed: second layer on red cap of wild mushrooms; Pintura white (01) + dab of Pintura cinnamon (52): bottom of cap and stalks of wild mushrooms; Pintura cinnamon (52): lines on bottom of cap of wild mushrooms, shadow on wild mushrooms, spots at the bottom of the stalks of the wild mushrooms, several blades of grass; Pintura yellow (16) + dab of Pintura green (08): several blades of grass; Pintura yellow ochre (05) + dab of Pintura orange (06) + dab of Pintura cinnamon (52): several leaves; Pintura yellow ochre (05) + dab of Pintura cinnamon (52): several leaves; Pintura brown (12): spots on bottom of stem of wild mushrooms; Tinta white (01T): dots on cap of wild mushrooms; Pintura cinnamon (52) and Pintura brown (12) mixed: small shadow lines below white dots on cap of wild mushrooms.

Dorsing (with Dorso oil)

Dorso brown (assort. 2): behind the leaves below the wild mushrooms.

Embossing

Wild mushrooms, leaves, card outline, all straight lines; alternating leaves in the border, one only the outline and the veins, then one leaf completely embossed. Take a good look at the colour example.

Finishing

Fold the card. Perforate deeply with the 2-needle tool according to pattern. Perforate shallowly with the 4-needle tool along the card outline and emboss dots between the 4-needle perforations. Perforate deeply with the 4-needle tool a second time along the card outline. Cut the 2-needle perforations out along the border of the front sheet and the back sheet. Cut the card out along the outer 4-needle perforations.

PURPLE TULIPS

General

The outer card and the extra front sheet are made of ivory Fantasy Parchment 2 (art.nr. 1477), the inner card is made of purple Fantasy Parchment 2 (art.nr. 1477). Other materials: mother-of-pearl embroidery thread.

Tracing

On extra front sheet: Tinta leaf green (10T): stems, leaves, inner line of small square around tulips and inner line of large square around tulips; Tinta purple (07T): tulips, buds, outer line of small square around tulips and outer line of large square around tulips.

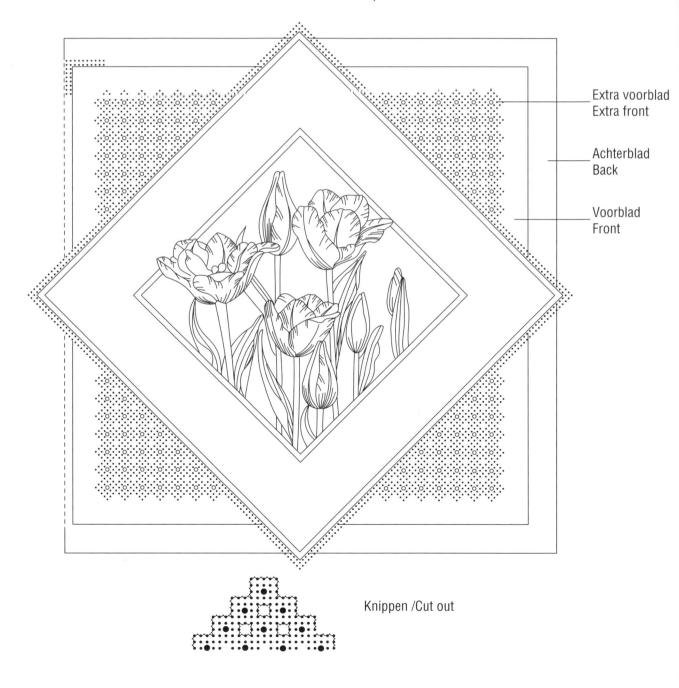

Extra voorblad
Extra front

Achterblad
Back

Voorblad
Front

Knippen /Cut out

On front sheet outer card: Tinta purple (07T): outline.

Painting

Tinta purple (07T) thinned with water: light parts of tulips; Tinta purple (07T): parts of tulips that are slightly darker; Pintura purple (07): shadow on tulips; Tinta leaf green (10T) thinned with water: light parts of leaves and stems; Tinta leaf green (10T): parts of leaves and stems that are slightly darker; Pintura green (08): shadow on leaves and stems.

Perforating (shallow)

With the 4-needle tool according to the pattern of the extra front sheet and along outline of front sheet outer card.

Embossing

Tulips, buds, leaves, stems, between double lines of small and large square, dots between 4-needle perforations along outline of extra front sheet and front sheet outer card, dots between perforation grid of extra front sheet according to pattern.

Perforating (deep)

With the 4-needle tool for a second time according to the pattern of the extra front sheet and along outline of front sheet outer card.

Cutting

Cut the 4-needle perforations according to the pattern; cut the front sheet of the outer card and the extra front sheet along the outer 4-needle perforations.

Finishing off

Fold the outer card and the inner card and thread them together along the fold line with the embroidery thread. Cut the inner card and the back sheet of the outer card off straight. Attach the extra front sheet on the front sheet of the outer card with a few stitches of embroidery thread between the 4-needle perforations.

PURPLE ANEMONE

General

The outer card is made of ordinary parchment paper and the inner card is made of light green Fantasy Parchment 2 (art.no. 1477). The lines technique was used to paint with Perga-Liners. Hold the brush upright and paint with the tip of the brush. Move the brush away from you. Paint fine lines and lift the brush slowly at the end of each line.

Tracing

Tinta white (01T): card outline of outer card and all straight lines.

Painting (with Perga-Liners)

B1, B5, A1, A6 and A7: petals; B1, B3, A1, A17 and A3: flower heart; B3 and A17: balls on stamens; A1: shiny spot on balls; A3: stamens and outline of balls on stamens.

Dorsing (with Dorso oil)

Dorso violet (assort. 1): between double lines of two square borders.

Perforating (shallow)

With perforating tool Flower Tool between double lines of borders according to pattern.

Embossing

Entire flower (emboss some petals on front), straight lines of square borders, between Flower Tool perforations according to pattern, and outline.

Perforating (deep)

With perforating tool Flower Tool a second time between double lines of borders according to pattern.

Cutting

Cut Flower Tool perforations out according to pattern.

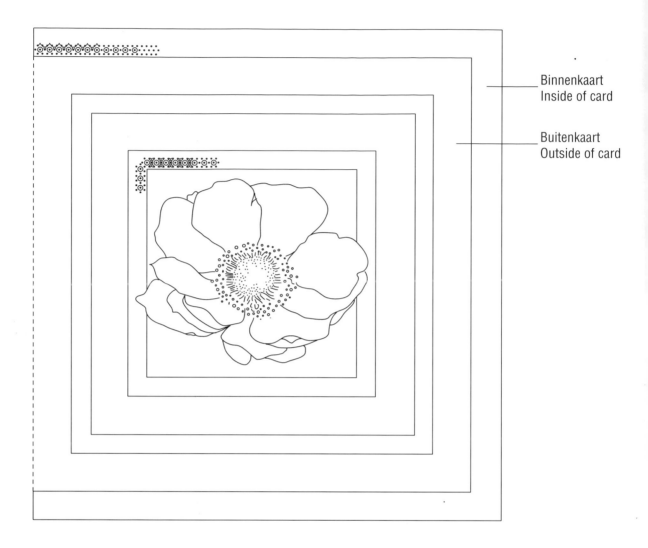

Binnenkaart
Inside of card

Buitenkaart
Outside of card

Knippen /Cut out

Finishing

Fold the outer card. Perforate shallowly with perforating tool Flower Tool along the card outline. Emboss with embossing tool Extra Small Ball between Flower Tool perforations according to pattern. Perforate deeply with the 1-needle tool in all holes of the Flower Tool perforations (perforating deeply with perforating tool Flower Tool through two layers of parchment paper puts too much pressure on the paper, which may cause the parchment paper to tear). Cut the card outline out along the outer Flower Tool perforations. Attach the inner card in the outer card and cut it off straight.

AZALEA

General

The card is made of lilac-coloured cardboard (Artoz) and the extra front sheet is made of ordinary parchment paper with an extra front sheet of lilac-coloured cardboard under it. A light pink sheet of paper has been attached between these two front sheets. Other materials: mother-of-pearl embroidery thread. The card is first embossed, then coloured in on the back with Perga Colors Exclusive, then shadow is applied on the front with Perga-Liners and Perga Colors Exclusive.

Tracing

Tinta gold (22T): entire picture (except all straight lines).

Extra voorblad van lilakleurig karton
Extra front of lilac card

Extra voorblad van gewoon perkamentpapier
Extra front of regular parchment paper

Borduren /Embroider

Knippen / Cut out

Embossing
Flowers, buds, leaves and stems.

Colouring in with Perga Colors Exclusive (on back)
PCE 6: flowers and buds; PCE 16: stems and leaves.

Perga-Liners (dry technique)
B6: apply a fine shadow lines on the darkest parts of the leaves where they have not been embossed.

Painting with Perga Colors Exclusive
PCE 6: apply fine shadow lines with brush on the darkest parts (e.g., from the flower heart; see colour example) of the flowers where they have not been embossed.

Finishing off
Perforate shallowly with the 4-needle tool and em-boss dots between these perforations according to pattern. Perforate deeply with the 2-needle and 4-needle tool according to pattern. Cut the extra front sheet of ordinary parchment paper along the 2-needle perforations and along the outer 4-needle perforations. Attach the light pink paper to the lilac-coloured extra front sheet with double-sided tape; temporarily attach the front sheet of ordinary parchment paper to this with Scotch tape. Use the 1-needle tool again to make perforations in the three holes that need to be embroidered (see embroidery example). Embroider extra front sheet of ordinary parchment paper on the lilac-coloured extra front sheet with the embroidery thread according to pattern. Fold the card and cut it off straight. Attach the entire extra front sheet to the card with double-sided foam tape.

ROSES

General
The outer card is made of ordinary parchment paper and the inner card is made of ivory Fantasy Parchment 2 (art.no. 1477). Other material: mother-of-pearl embroidery thread.
The card is first embossed, then coloured in on the back with Perga Colors Exclusive, then shadow is applied on the front with Perga-Liners.

Tracing
Tinta black (11T): entire picture in border; Tinta white (01T): card outline, all straight lines and pictures between card outline and border.

Embossing
Entire picture in border, pictures between card outline and border, all straight lines and very lightly between inner two lines of border.

Colouring in with Perga Colors Exclusive (on back)
PCE 5: roses in border; PCE 2: flower heart of bottom right rose; PCE 15: several leaves and stems; PCE16: several leaves.

Perga-Liners (dry technique)
B3 and B11: apply shadow on the front on the darkest parts of the roses where they have not been embossed.

Stippling
With 1-needle tool: between inner lines of border.

Finishing
Fold the inner card and the outer card. Thread the cards together along the fold line with the embroidery thread. Perforate shallowly with perforating tool Semi-Square along the card outline (through all four layers). Emboss dots between the Semi-Square perforations according to pattern. Perforate deeply with the 1-needle tool in all holes of the Semi-Square perforations (this is to prevent the parchment paper from tearing). Cut the inner card and the outer card out layer by layer along the outer Semi-Square perforations.

GIFT TAG ROSE

General
The card is made of ordinary parchment paper and the insert card is made of soft pink cardboard. The card is first embossed, then coloured in on the back with Perga Colors Exclusive, then shadow is applied on the front with Perga-Liners.

Tracing
Tinta white (01T): card outline, all straight lines; Tinta black (11T): entire picture.

Dorsing (with Dorso oil)
Dorso red (assort. 2): between outline and outer border.

Perforating (shallow)
With Semi-Square perforating tool along card outline according to pattern.

Embossing
(Shadow embossing: short and long lines beside each other with embossing tools Large Ball and Small Ball, avoid embossing too much, because everything that is white stays white – take a good look at the

example). Bud and all rose leaves only from outer rim to inside, leaves, flower hearts, balls on stamens, dots between Semi-Square perforations according to pattern, card outline, all straight lines and very light between the inner double straight lines.

Colouring in with Perga Colors Exclusive (on back)

PCE 7: roses; PCE 15: stems and leaves; PCE 2: flower hearts and balls on stamens.

Perga-Liners (dry technique)

Apply shadow on the front on the darkest parts where it has not been embossed. B11: roses.

Stippling

With 1-needle tool: between inner double straight lines.

Perforating (deep)

With Semi-Square perforating tool again along card outline according to pattern.

Cutting

Cut the card out along the outer Semi-Square perforations.

Finishing off

Fold the card. Attach the insert sheet in the card with narrow strips of double-sided tape.

ROSE

General

The card is made of ordinary parchment paper and the insert card is made of soft-pink cardboard. The card is first embossed, then coloured in on the back with Perga Colors Exclusive, then shadow is applied on the front with Perga-Liners.

Tracing

Tinta gold (22T): card outline and all straight lines; Tinta black (11T): entire picture and leaves and stems in the border.

Embossing

(Shadow embossing: short and long lines beside each other with embossing tools Large Ball and Small Ball; avoid embossing too much, because everything that is white stays white – take a good look at the example.)

All petals (only from the outer border inwards), a very small line on the stem, leaves, small leaves in the border and very lightly between double lines in the border.

Colouring in with Perga Colors Exclusive (on back)
PCE 7: rose; PCE 15: stem and all leaves; PCE 2: flower heart.

Perga-Liners (dry technique)
Apply shadow on the front on the darkest parts where it has not been embossed. B3 and B11: rose; B6: leaves.

Stippling
With 1-needle tool: flower heart and between double lines in the border.

Perforating
With 2-needle tool along part of leaf on left side of fold line.

Cutting
Cut out 2-needle perforations along part of leaf of left side of fold line.

Finishing
Fold the card. Attach the insert card in the card with double-sided Scotch tape. Perforate with the 2-needle tool along the card outline and cut the card and the insert card out along these perforations.

1) Result after embossing

2) Colouring with PCE on back

3) Result after colouring with PCE

4) Dry technique with Perga-Liners Basic on front

KINGFISHER (pattern on page 5)

General

The outer card is made of Parchment Vellum daisies (art.no. 1620) and the inner card is made of ordinary parchment paper on which the kingfisher is painted. Other material: gold-coloured embroidery thread.

Tracing

On outer card: Tinta orange (06T): double outlines and double lines of square.

On inner card: Tinta blue (02T): head and back; Tinta orange (06T): stomach and bottom of tail; Tinta sepia (12T): beak, white spots on kingfisher and tree-stump; Tinta black (11T): eye.

Painting

Tinta blue (02T): head and back; Pintura blue (02) + Pintura brown (12): fine lines to suggest feathers on head and back of bird; Tinta white (01T): spots on head, spot below beak, spot next to eye,

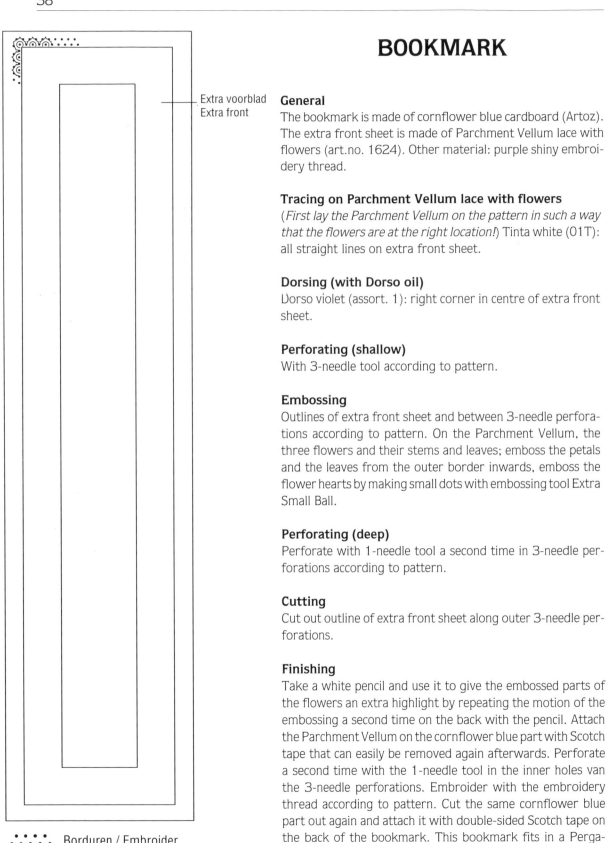

Extra voorblad
Extra front

BOOKMARK

General
The bookmark is made of cornflower blue cardboard (Artoz). The extra front sheet is made of Parchment Vellum lace with flowers (art.no. 1624). Other material: purple shiny embroidery thread.

Tracing on Parchment Vellum lace with flowers
(*First lay the Parchment Vellum on the pattern in such a way that the flowers are at the right location!*) Tinta white (01T): all straight lines on extra front sheet.

Dorsing (with Dorso oil)
Dorso violet (assort. 1): right corner in centre of extra front sheet.

Perforating (shallow)
With 3-needle tool according to pattern.

Embossing
Outlines of extra front sheet and between 3-needle perforations according to pattern. On the Parchment Vellum, the three flowers and their stems and leaves; emboss the petals and the leaves from the outer border inwards, emboss the flower hearts by making small dots with embossing tool Extra Small Ball.

Perforating (deep)
Perforate with 1-needle tool a second time in 3-needle perforations according to pattern.

Cutting
Cut out outline of extra front sheet along outer 3-needle perforations.

Finishing
Take a white pencil and use it to give the embossed parts of the flowers an extra highlight by repeating the motion of the embossing a second time on the back with the pencil. Attach the Parchment Vellum on the cornflower blue part with Scotch tape that can easily be removed again afterwards. Perforate a second time with the 1-needle tool in the inner holes van the 3-needle perforations. Embroider with the embroidery thread according to pattern. Cut the same cornflower blue part out again and attach it with double-sided Scotch tape on the back of the bookmark. This bookmark fits in a Pergamano bookmark cover (art.no. 1174).

CORNFLOWER BLUE CARD WITH 3-D BUTTERFLY

General

The card is made of cornflower blue cardboard (Artoz). The extra front sheet is made of Parchment Vellum lace with flowers (art.no. 1624). 3-D ele-ment: butterfly (2x), one of ordinary parchment paper and one of cornflower blue cardboard. Other material: mother-of-pearl embroidery thread, nylon thread (2x 5cm).

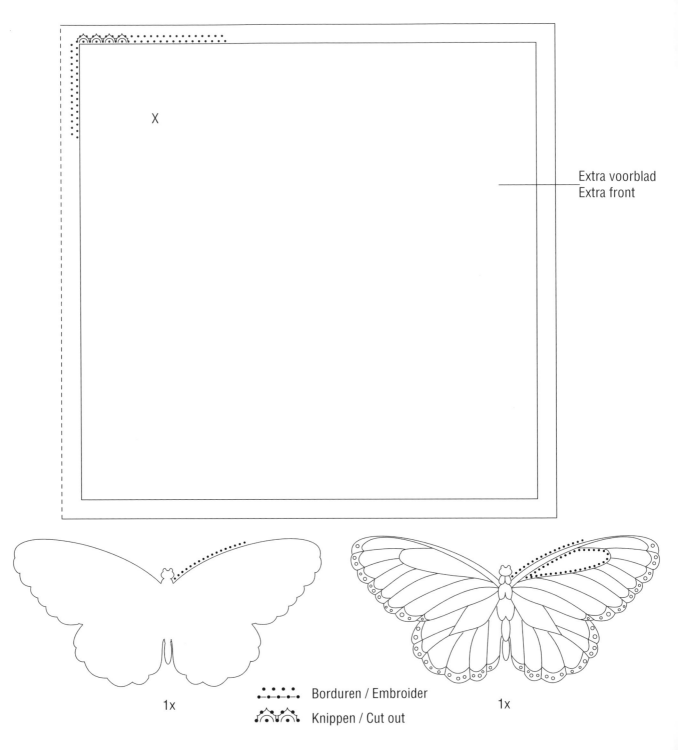

X

Extra voorblad
Extra front

1x

•·•·•· Borduren / Embroider

Knippen / Cut out

1x

Tracing on Parchment Vellum lace with flowers

(*First position the Vellum on the pattern in such a way that the flowers are at the right locations!*) Tinta white (01T): card outline.

Tracing on ordinary parchment paper

Tinta white (01T): butterfly; Tinta Pearl violet (= Tinta Pearl red (03TP) and Tinta Pearl blue (02TP) mixed): dots on outer border of wings of butterfly.

Perforating (shallow)

With 3-needle tool according to pattern.

Embossing

Areas along outer border of wings of butterfly (very lightly), butterfly, card outline and between 3-needle perforations according to pattern. On the Parchment Vellum the grass, the two flowers and their stems and leaves; emboss the petals and the leaves from the outer border inwards and also from the inside outwards a very little bit, emboss the flower hearts by creating small dots with embossing tool Extra Small Ball.

Stippling

With 1-needle tool: areas along outer border of wings of butterfly.

Perforating (deep)

Attach the butterfly on the cornflower blue cardboard and perforate with the 2-needle tool along the outline of the butterfly. Remove the cornflower blue butterfly and perforate the parchment paper butterfly with the 2-needle tool according to pattern. Perforate with 1-needle tool a second time in 3-needle perforations according to pattern.

Cutting

Cut the 3-D butterflies out; cut outline of extra front sheet out along outer 3-needle perforations.

Finishing

Take a white pencil and use it to give the embossed parts of the flowers an extra highlight by repeating the motion of the embossing a second time on the back with the pencil. Turn the Parchment Vellum over, use a Perga-Liner B5 and apply shadow below the flowers and draw a straight line on the inside of the white card outline. Attach the Parchment Vellum on the card with Scotch tape that can easily be removed again. Perforate a second time with the 1-needle tool in the inner holes of the 3-needle perforations. Embroider with the embroidery thread according to pattern. Fold the card and cut it off straight. Make antennae for the butterfly. Take two 5-cm pieces of nylon thread. Dip them in Tinta white (01T) and allow to dry, now dip the ends of the nylon threads several times in Pintura white (01) and allow to dry. Attach the antennae with Pergakit below the body of the parchment paper butterfly and allow to dry. Attach the cornflower blue butterfly on the card (location marker 'x'). Attach the parchment paper butterfly with a dab of Pergakit on the cornflower blue butterfly.

3-D BUTTERFLY IN SQUARE

General

The outer card is made of Parchment Vellum lace (art.no. 1624) and the inner card is made of cornflower blue cardboard paper (Artoz). 3-D element: butterfly (1x) of ordinary parchment paper. Other material: mother-of-pearl embroidery thread, nylon thread (2x 4cm).

Tracing on Parchment Vellum lace

Tinta white (01T): entire picture.

Tracing on ordinary parchment paper

Tinta white (01T): 3-D butterfly.

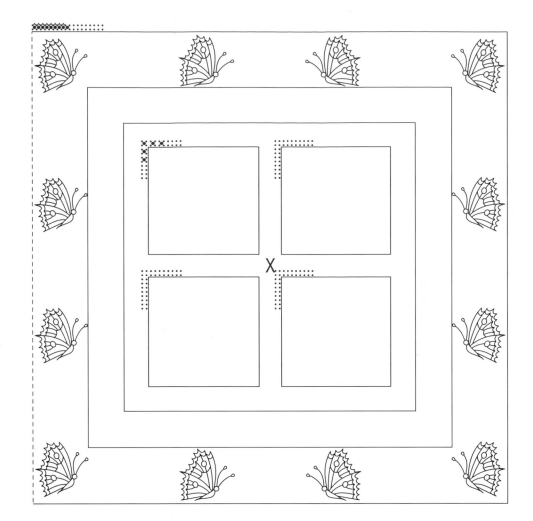

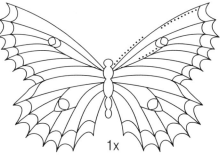

1x

Dorsing (with Dorso oil)

Dorso violet (assort. 1): between double lines of outer border and square at top right; Dorso lilac (assort. 2): square at top left; Dorso fuchsia (assort. 1): square at bottom left; Dorso blue (assort. 1): square at bottom right.

Perforating (shallow)

With 4-needle tool according to pattern.

Embossing

Areas along outer border of wings of 3-D butterfly (very lightly), 3-D butterfly, all straight lines and dots between 4-needle perforations according to pattern. With 1-needle tool very carefully (hold the tool at a very slanted angle and move it towards you while embossing) small butterflies in border.

Stippling

With 1-needle tool: areas along outer border of wings of 3-D butterfly.

Perforating (deep)

With 2-needle tool, 3-D butterfly according to pattern; with 1-needle tool a second time in all 4-needle perforations.

Cutting

Cut 3-D butterfly out; cut card outline out along outer 4-needle perforations.

Finishing

Fold the inner card and the outer card and thread them on the fold line together with the embroidery thread. Cut the inner card and the back sheet of the outer card off straight. Make antennae for the but- terfly. Take two 4-cm pieces of nylon thread. Dip them in the Tinta white (01T) and allow them to dry; now dip the ends of the nylon threads several times in Pintura white (01) and allow to dry. Attach the antennae under the body of the butterfly with Pergakit and allow to dry. Attach the butterfly in the centre of the card with a dab of Pergakit (loca- tion 'x').

CUCKOOFLOWERS

General

The card is made of ordinary parchment paper and the insert card is made of dark red card- board. 3-D elements: small flow- ers (19x) of Parchment Vellum Flower Fairies no. 5 (art.no. 1628).

Tracing

Tinta bordeaux (= Tinta red (03T) and very little Tinta black (11T) mixed): cuckooflowers and double outlines; Tinta leaf green (10T): stems and leaves.

Painting

Tinta bordeaux thinned with water: flowers; Tinta bordeaux: about half the blocks on the flow- ers alternating; Pintura bordeaux (51): shadow on flowers; Pintu- ra yellow (16) + dab of Pintura green (08): stems and leaves.

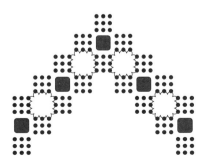

Perforating

With Easy-Grid fine mesh and perforating tool Arrow according to pattern.

Embossing

Cuckooflowers, stems, leaves, squares between Easy-Grid perforations and very lightly between double outlines.

Stippling

With 1-needle tool: between double outlines.

Cutting

Cut Easy-Grid perforations out according to pattern.

Finishing

Fold the card. Attach the insert card in the card with narrow strips of double-sided Scotch tape. Perforate with the 1-needle tool along the outer border of the parts that protrude from the card and with the 2-needle tool along the rest of the card outline through all layers. Cut the card out along these perforations. Cut 19 small flowers out of the Parchment Vellum Flower Fairies, emboss them and attach them on the card with a dab of Pergakit (see colour example for instructions on where to put them).

General

The inner card and the outer card are made of ordinary parchment paper. Other material: mother-of-pearl embroidery thread. The card is first embossed, then coloured in on the back with Perga Colors Exclusive and lastly shadows are applied on the front with Perga-Liners.

Tracing

On outer card: Tinta black (11T): entire picture van blue grapes; Tinta white (01T): only left outline right next to line.
On inner card: Tinta white (01T): double outlines.

Perforating

On outer card: with Easy-Grid fine mesh and perforating tool Arrow according to pattern.

Embossing

On outer card: dots between Easy-Grid perforations according to pattern, blue grapes, (very lightly) stems and leaves.
On inner card: (very lightly) between double outlines.

Colouring in with Perga Colors Exclusive (on back)

PCE 10: blue grapes; PCE 16 and PCE 15: stems and leaves.

Perga-Liners (dry technique)

B5: apply shadow on the front on the darkest parts van the small flowers where they are not embossed.

Perga-Liners (rub out with Dorso oil)

Place the inner card on the pattern with the good side down. Apply B6 and B5 alternately at the location of the perforated squares in the border. Attach Scotch tape around the squares so the edges of the squares stay nice. Rub the colour out with very little Dorso oil. Remove the Scotch tape.

Cutting

Cut Easy-Grid perforations out according to pattern; cut card outline of the front sheet of the outer card out along the outer Easy-Grid perforations.

Finishing

Fold the inner card and the outer card. Thread the cards on the fold line together with the embroidery thread. Perforate with the 2-needle tool along the card outline, penetrating through the three layers in one try. Cut the card out along the 2-needle perforations layer by layer.

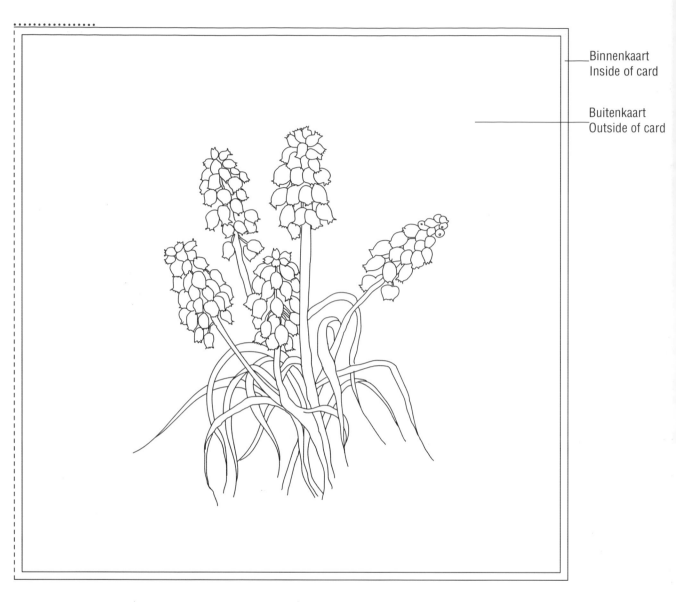

Binnenkaart
Inside of card

Buitenkaart
Outside of card

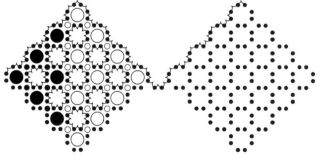

ORCHID

General
The card is made of ordinary parchment paper and the insert card is made of pink paper. The lines technique was used to paint with Perga-Liners. Hold the brush upright and paint with the tip of the brush. Move the brush away from you. Paint fine lines and lift the brush slowly at the end of each line.

Achterblad
Back

Voorblad
Front

Tracing
Tinta white (01T): double outlines of border, orchids between border and card outline; Tinta leaf
green (10T): stem and leaves; Tinta sepia (12T):
red petals.

Painting (with Perga-Liners)
B1 and A1: white part in flower heart; A17: spots
on white part in flower heart; A3: outline of white
part in flower heart; B8, A20, A19, A15 and A17:
yellow/green part in centre of orchid; B1, B11, B10,
A10, A8, A17 and very little A3: red petals; B1,B7,
B6, A1, A15 and A16: leaves and stem.

Embossing
All orchids, stems, leaves, card outline and very lightly between double lines of borders.

Stippling
With 1-needle tool: between double lines of borders.

Finishing
Perforate shallowly with the 3-needle tool along the
outline of the front sheet. Emboss between the
3-needle perforations according to pattern. Perforate a second time, deeply now, with the 3-needle
tool and cut the front sheet out along these perforations. Fold the card. Attach the insert card in the
card with double-sided Scotch tape. Cut the insert
card and the back sheet off straight (about 3mm
larger than the front sheet).